THE
GHOSTLY TALES
OF
THE BERKSHIRES

T0016789

These ghostly tales are dedicated to
Mrs. Carpenter's third-grade class at Rectory
School in Pomfret, CT, with gratitude.

—Mr. Oakes

Published by Arcadia Children's Books
A Division of Arcadia Publishing
Charleston, SC
www.arcadiapublishing.com

Spooky America is a trademark of Arcadia Publishing, Inc.

First published 2023

Manufactured in the United States

ISBN: 978-1-4671-9736-6

Library of Congress Control Number 2023937847

Notice: The information in this book is true and complete to the best of our
knowledge. It is offered without guarantee on the part of the author or Arcadia
Publishing. The author and Arcadia Publishing disclaim all liability in connection with
the use of this book.

Illustrations by Katherine Oakes
Images used courtesy of Shutterstock.com.

Spooky America

THE GHOSTLY TALES OF THE BERKSHIRES

ROBERT OAKES

ILLUSTRATIONS BY KATHERINE OAKES

Adapted from *Ghosts of the Berkshires* by Robert Oakes

arcadia
CHILDREN'S BOOKS

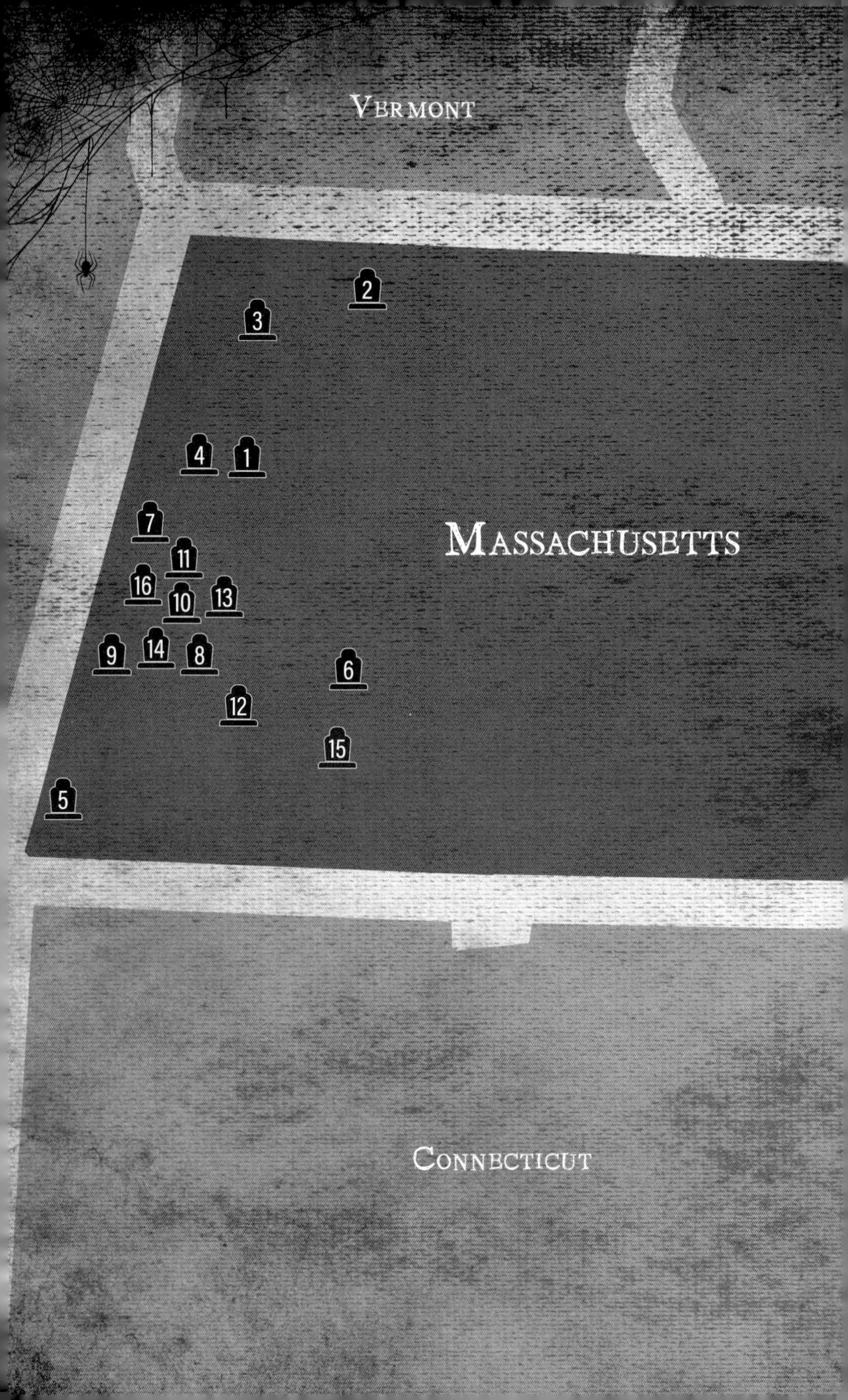

Vermont
2
3
4
1
7
Massachusetts
11
16
10
13
9
14
8
6
12
15
5
Connecticut

Table of Contents & Map Key

Join Me If You Dare!

If I invited you to join me on a walk through a dark, haunted house, would you go? What if we had flashlights to light our way? Would you say yes?

For years now, I have done that very thing. I have led ghost tours through two of the Berkshires's most haunted estates, The Mount and Ventfort Hall. Week after week, I take folks to rooms where the shadows seem to move. I lead them down hallways where soft whispers have been heard. I show them haunted dolls, an eerie stable, and photos of faces in windows, and I tell them tales of the strange and spooky things that others have experienced in these places. Along the way, we shine our lights into the darkness, pushing away the shadows as we go. And we wonder what might be in the unseen spaces beyond our beams of light.

And we are not alone. For years, people who have lived here in the Berkshires have wondered what might be lurking out among the hills. This wild and wooded county on the far western side of Massachusetts has inspired story upon story of sinister spirits and mysterious creatures. These stories were told by the Mohicans, who once called this land their home, as well as by the European settlers of the colonial days. They were shared by the farmers, woodcutters, and millworkers of the nineteenth century, as well as by the wealthy tycoons who built their grand estates. Up to this very day, the tourists, vacationers, and visitors who enjoy this special place continue to encounter the ghosts of the Berkshires and have many tales to tell—tales that I can't wait to share with you.

So join me, if you dare, on this walk through the shadows of the Berkshires. Listen as I tell you about some of the eerie things that people here have seen and heard and felt. And if you get scared, remember the flashlight that you have. Ghosts may be hiding in the shadows, but that beam of light will always scare them off.

You'd Better Watch Your Step at Wizard's Glen

In the town of Dalton, Massachusetts, there is a rocky dirt road that winds through trees and heaps of stones. It's called Gulf Road because about 150 years ago, this area was known as the Gulf. It probably got that name because of the tall slopes of tumbled stones that surround people on all sides as they walk through. People used to go there for picnics or to take walks in the woods. By that time, people had forgotten all about the monsters and ghosts that the early settlers of the Berkshires believed haunted this place. Those early settlers called this wild and wooded area the "Wizard's Glen." They thought of it as an evil place. Everyone was told to stay away, and everyone heeded the warning—except a man named John Chamberlain.

Returning from a day of hunting one afternoon, Chamberlain decided to take a shortcut through the Glen. A terrible storm was coming, and he wanted to get home before it reached him. He made it about halfway through the Glen before the storm clouds burst. Rain, wind, thunder, and lightning roared through the trees overhead. Chamberlain slid beneath a giant stone beside the road and waited for the storm to pass. He waited and waited, but it only got worse.

Then he saw a horrible sight. Not far from him, hundreds of creatures came walking through the woods, carrying torches that burned with a pale blue light. There were demons with hooved feet and others with batlike wings. There were vampires, werewolves, goblins, and ghosts. Chamberlain gasped. Never in his life had he felt so afraid. The monsters and ghosts passed only a few feet from where he lay and then tramped into the woods beside him. And then there came the biggest and most terrifying monster of all. This one had horns and a long, spiked tail. Chamberlain almost gave himself away by screaming, but somehow he managed to stay quiet.

All at once, the creatures began to chant as they dragged a frightened young woman out of the shadows and moved in close to do her harm. Chamberlain decided that he must do something to help her, even though he was afraid. So, he reached for the Bible he had tucked away in his pocket. He burst out from his hiding place, shouting a prayer. When they saw the holy book and heard the holy words, the monsters and ghosts, as well as the woman, suddenly disappeared, and the pale blue light went out. Alone in the dark, Chamberlain lay down under the stone and fell asleep. In the morning when he woke, everything had returned to normal. It was as if nothing strange had happened the night before. Was it only a dream? Maybe. Who can say for sure?

If you visit Wizard's Glen today, you'll find a sign beside the road that reads, "Use at your own risk." Just like John Chamberlain all those years ago, travelers today would be wise to heed that warning. If you dare go down Gulf Road, you'd better watch your step!

A Journey through the Hoosac Tunnel

As the train approached the tunnel, the gray-haired engineer throttled the engine down until it moved at a slow crawl. The younger man who sat beside him, an engineer-in-training, looked at the old man curiously.

"Why did you slow us down?" he asked.

"This is the Hoosac Tunnel," said the old man, thinking that the name alone would explain it. But the younger man just shrugged.

"You've never heard of the Hoosac Tunnel? The Bloody Pit? The Tunnel from Hell?" asked the engineer.

"I can't say I have," replied the young trainee.

They passed into the shadow of the mountain as the inky black tunnel opened wide like a mouth about to swallow them.

"I hate this part of the line," said the old man. "It gives me the creeps."

"It's just a tunnel," the young man said. "We've been through dozens of them."

"Not like this one. This one is cursed. Bad things happen in there. People get killed. And there are ghosts."

"Ghosts?" said the younger man. "Come on. There's no such thing."

"Oh, yes, there is," the old man said. "You just wait and see."

Just then, the train entered the tunnel, and total darkness surrounded them as if someone had turned out the light. Cold, clammy air entered the car through an open window making the young man shiver in spite of himself. As his eyes adjusted to the dark, he looked up at the tunnel walls on either side and overhead. He saw where the neatly cut blocks of stone near the tunnel's entrance turned to rough rock that looked like some kind of creature had dug it out with huge, sharp claws.

"When did they build this place?" he asked the older man.

"They started it in 1851," replied the engineer. "They thought it would take only a few years to build, but they didn't get it done until 1875. Twenty-four years. Twenty-four years of sheer hell. Explosions, collapses, floods: the men who worked here saw it all. Out of the eight hundred men who built it, two hundred of them died in here. And even back then, people said those men who died came back as ghosts to haunt the ones who lived. They said they heard voices coming from somewhere in the dark, and they started to get too scared to go back in. Their bosses tried to tell them it was only the wind coming through the tunnel, but the men wouldn't have it. They knew a voice when they heard one."

"I'm surprised they didn't quit," said the younger man.

"Some of them probably did," the engineer replied. "But most of them stayed on. These were some pretty tough guys, you know, and anyway, they needed the work. But, boy, was it dangerous. Especially when they started using explosives to

blow their way through. Some of the men died when the rock collapsed on top of them. Two men—Ned Brinkman and Billy Nash, were buried under tons of rock when a man named Ringo Kelley set off an explosive too soon. A year after that accident, Kelley was found dead in the same place where it had happened. They never found out what caused his death. But people said the angry ghosts of Brinkman and Nash killed him to get him back for the accident.

"Then there was the big explosion in the shaft that ran up from the tunnel to the mountaintop. Thirteen men died that day. For a year afterward, local residents said they could see their ghosts walking through the woods toward the opening with pickaxes over their shoulder, as if they were still on their way to work."

"People say all kinds of things," the young man said. "That doesn't make it true. I've never seen a ghost, and until I do, I'm not about to believe in them."

"How do you know you haven't seen one?" the old man asked. "Some people don't know they've seen a ghost until after they've seen it. You may have talked to a ghost and not even known it."

There was a long pause as the train wheels screeched loudly on the tracks.

"For all you know," the old man continued, "*I* could be a ghost."

The young man laughed. "For all you know, so could I," he replied.

"There is one more story about this tunnel," the engineer said. "It's about a ghost train they say rides these tracks. It was a foggy night long ago when a freight train was traveling west through the tunnel. Something went wrong, some wires got crossed somewhere, and another train was sent eastbound through the tunnel on the very same stretch of track. There was a terrible collision and many people died. Some say that on certain days, any train heading west through the tunnel will see the oncoming light of the ghost train, and they'll see the ghost of the engineer who died at the wheel that night."

"You're making that up," the young man said. "That never happened. You're just trying to scare me."

Suddenly, a bright light appeared on the tracks ahead of them. It started out small but quickly grew bigger and brighter until it filled the engine car with light. There was the screeching of wheels and the smell of diesel fuel.

"Watch out!" the young man screamed as he held his hands over his eyes. He braced for impact, but it never came. Instead, a chill passed through his body as if he had dived into a pool of icy water. Then, suddenly, all was quiet again as the train passed out of the tunnel and back out toward the setting sun. The young man took a deep breath and looked at the seat beside him, saying, "Wow, that was close."

But he was surprised to find the gray-haired engineer was gone.

The Old Coot of Mount Greylock

On a mountain known as Greylock by a place called Bascom Lodge, there was a crowd around a fire on a dark and foggy night.

"Many tales are told about this mountain," said a bearded old man with a gravelly voice as he tossed another log onto the fire. It landed with a shower of sparks that rose into the air, where they mingled with the fireflies and stars. "Someone once said that the fairies used to dance here in these grassy glades. A famous author named Herman Melville, who wrote the book *Moby Dick*, thought this entire mountain was a huge whale rising from the sea. And another one called J.K. Rowling, of *Harry Potter* fame, imagined a North American school of wizardry up here above the clouds. But the *best-known* tale about Mount Greylock is the story of the Old Coot, a sad and lonely spirit said to haunt the woods near the Bellows Pipe and Thunderbolt Trails.

"But he wasn't always known as the Old Coot," said the old man, "and he wasn't always so lonely and sad. When he was young, his name was William Saunders, or Bill for short. He was a farmer who lived with his wife, Belle, along with their children, by the slopes of the mountain. This was back in the 1860s, during the days of the Civil War, when the northern and southern parts of our country were at war with one another. Like so many young men at that time, Bill was called to fight. So, he left his wife and children to tend the farm alone and marched off to the war, not knowing if he would ever come back.

"Months later, Belle received news that Bill had been badly hurt. Though she waited and waited for almost a year, she heard nothing more about him. Belle assumed that the worst had happened. Her husband must have died. So, she married another man—a new husband for her, a new father for their children. And the newly mended family moved on.

One day, years later, a grizzled man in a worn-out army uniform arrived in town. It was Bill Saunders, home at last from war. But he looked so different from the fresh-faced young man who had marched off years before that no one in town knew who he was. He was thinner and paler and looked much older. He had a limp that was caused by a wound on his leg. Bill shambled up to his old farm and leaned against the gate. There, he saw his children call this other man "Daddy." He saw his wife kissing her new husband. Bill didn't want to spoil their happy new life, so he decided not to tell them he was back. Instead, he built a little cabin further up the mountain and lived there all alone.

People in town started calling him the strange "Old Coot," especially when they saw him wandering in the woods by the Bellows Pipe. During the long, cold winter months, Bill sat beside his wood stove, keeping warm and waiting for spring. But during one very cold night in late January, a blast of wind blew open his door, putting out the fire. Bill froze to death that night in his sleep. Days later, some hunters came to the cabin. They were shocked to discover Bill's frozen body inside. The hunters also found some papers with

Bill's name on them. That's how they knew that this frozen man was poor old Bill Saunders, who had lived among them all those years, unrecognized. Just as they were about to call the police, the men shrieked. They saw Bill's ghost rise up from his body, pass right through the wall, and limp away into the woods.

"Ever since that day, many people say the ghost of the Old Coot still limps along near the intersection of the Bellows Pipe and Thunderbolt Trails, especially at the end of January, about the time of year he died. Sometimes, they say, if he finds a campfire, he'll shamble over to it to warm himself with the heat of the flames and the company of friends. So, while you're up here on Mount Greylock, keep your eyes open for the Old Coot's ghost. He may be there with you, though you don't even know it."

As the old man finished his tale, he tossed another log on the fire, wished his audience a good night, and then limped away into the Greylock fog.

Ghost Boats on Pontoosuc Lake

If you walk along Pontoosuc Lake as the sun sets and the stars appear, you might see something strange out on the water: a ghost boat paddled by a shadowy boatman. No one knows who this might be or what he might be looking for. But back and forth he goes from dusk till dawn. This isn't the only ghost said to sail Pontoosuc Lake. Out there on the misty waves, two others may also be rowing, a pair of young Mohicans known as Moon-keek and Shoon-keek.

According to an old Berkshire legend, Moon-keek and Shoon-keek wanted to be close but were told to keep apart. Because they were cousins, they were not allowed to marry. But because they were in love, they didn't listen. Every night, they went together to the woods to be alone. But what they didn't know was that another young man was with them, always hiding in the shadows, always watching where they went. His name was Nock-a-wan-do. He was jealous of Shoon-keek, because he, too, was in love with beautiful Moon-keek. As he listened to them speaking words of love to one another, his mind grew dark with angry, jealous thoughts.

One night, while Nock-a-wan-do listened, Moon-keek and Shoon-keek made a plan to run away to another village where they would be allowed to marry.

"We'll each take a boat," said Shoon-keek, "and row out to the island in the middle of the lake. From there, we'll go together side-by-side."

"But what if they catch us?" Moon-keek asked. "Or what if one of us falls behind? I couldn't live without you."

"We must vow to stay together no matter what happens," answered Shoon-keek. "Nothing must keep us apart."

And so, they vowed. But Nock-a-wan-do *also* made a vow. He vowed to murder Shoon-keek before he reached the island, so that he might have Moon-keek all to himself. Before long, when the night came for Moon-keek and Shoon-keek

to escape across the lake, Nock-a-wan-do was there, too, hiding in the shadows. And as the two young lovers set out in their boats, the jealous Nock-a-wan-do shot an arrow from his bow, piercing Shoon-keek through the heart. The young man's body slumped over the side of the boat and sank beneath the lake. Moon-keek screamed out, "Shoon-keek," as she paddled her canoe toward his. Then, suddenly, she stopped. The ghost of Shoon-keek was there in his boat, arms folded and eyes staring straight ahead. As his boat passed her by, she heard his voice call out, "Moon-keek. Follow me, Moon-keek."

Moon-keek remembered her vow.

No matter what happens, nothing must keep us apart.

So, she stood up in her boat, jumped into the lake, and drowned. Then, Moon-keek's ghost also appeared in her canoe, and the two ghosts rowed together side-by-side.

From the shadows on the shore, Nock-a-wan-do saw the two canoes and heard their ghostly voices calling out: "Shoon-keek, Moon-keek, Shoon-keek, Moon-keek." Terrified, he ran back to the village and hid. He never went back to the lake, and he never told a soul about what he'd seen there that night—nor what he had done.

People say they still hear the voices of Moon-keek and Shoon-keek on Pontoosuc Lake, and sometimes they see their spirits out there, paddling side-by-side. Nothing—not even death— could tear the two apart.

CHAPTER 5

The Butterflies of Bash Bish Falls

Teagan turned the corner quickly as she followed a colorful butterfly.

"There's another one up here!" she called back to her mother, who was trying to keep up.

"Be careful, Teagan," her mother called. "Don't get too close to the falls."

"There are so many, Mom. Look!"

Stepping around a large boulder, Teagan's mom saw hundreds of butterflies fluttering all around the little girl. She walked into the space between the boulders and sat down beside her daughter on a large, flat stone.

"You know," she said. "There's a story about the butterflies here at Bash Bish Falls. Do you want to hear it?"

"Yes!" said Teagan. She sat down on the stone and felt the spray of water from the falls on her face. It felt cool in the heat of the early summer sun. As Teagan watched the butterfly wings glimmer in the golden light, her mother began the story.

"Long ago, the Mohican people lived here, and although they often came to the river to draw water, they would stay far away from the falls. They believed it was haunted by the ghost of a water witch called Bash Bish.

"When she was alive, Bash Bish was a beautiful young woman whom everybody loved, except for one other young woman who was jealous of her. This other woman started telling stories about

Bash Bish, saying that she had broken the rules of their community. Those in charge believed the stories and planned to punish Bash Bish by sending her over the falls in a canoe.

But on the day when they brought the young woman to the falls to be punished, an amazing thing happened. As she stood at the edge, about to be pushed over, she was suddenly surrounded by sunlight and hundreds of beautiful butterflies. They fluttered all around her. There were so many that all those who gathered near the falls to watch could hardly see the young woman. And they were all afraid because they thought this was the magic of witchcraft. Then, all at once, the butterflies started to fly away, and everyone was amazed because when the butterflies had vanished, Bash Bish was also gone.

"They never saw Bash Bish alive again, but they believed her spirit was in the falls. Some said they saw her face in the water. Others said they heard her voice in its splashes and crashes, whispering her name over and over again, 'Bash Bish, Bash Bish, Bash Bish.' They said she was a witch and stayed far away from the falls, afraid that she would curse them if they ever came too close.

"Bash Bish had a daughter named White Swan, who grew up to become one of the most beautiful women in the village, just like her mother had been. And when the time came, it was arranged for White Swan to marry the chief's son, Whirling Wind. But they never told Whirling Wind that his bride was the daughter of the water witch. They kept it a secret because they thought he would be too afraid to marry her if he knew. At first, Whirling Wind and White Swan were happy together, but after some time, White Swan became pale and thin and began to leave the village in the middle of the night.

"One night, Whirling Wind decided to follow her to find out where she was going. And as he heard the sound of the water growing closer and closer, he knew his wife was heading for the forbidden falls. When he reached the clearing beside the water, he saw her standing on the rocks, lit up by the moon. And he heard her speaking to the water below, 'Mother, I am here. Take me with you.' And suddenly, a milky white arm reached out of the falls and took his wife by the hand. And that's when he knew the secret the elders had kept from him all this time. His wife was the daughter of the water witch! He ran to her to try to pull her away from the falls, but he was too late! By the time Whirling Wind reached her, White Swan was gone.

"From that day on, people have said they see two ghosts in the twin waterfalls, one of Bash Bish and the other of her daughter, White Swan. And, they say, that whenever you see the butterflies fluttering over the water, it's a sign that the spirits of mother and daughter are there, happily together forever in the falls."

CHAPTER 6

The Haunted Stones in the Becket Quarry

Out near the town of Becket, there is a place filled with rusty old machinery surrounded by trees and stones. Today, it is called the Becket Land Trust Historic Quarry and Forest, where people go to hike or cross-country ski.

But long ago, this land was used as a quarry, where men pulled heavy stones out of the ground using explosives, drills, winches, trucks, and other kinds of equipment. The rock they mined there was used to make monuments and even tombstones, and the quarry was a very successful business for many years. But one day in the 1960s, the men who worked there walked off the job and never came back. They simply parked their trucks, dropped their tools, and went home. The quarry had closed forever.

If you go there today, you'll find the tools and equipment still rusting away in the woods. Trucks, winches, cables, and sheds—all of it is still there, just where the workmen left it. You'll also see large piles of stones that they dug out of the ground. And at the center of the property, you'll find a small pond. That is the heart of the old quarry. It was once the pit where they dug out the rock, but now it is filled with water.

If you do go to the old quarry, be warned. People say that it isn't only the quarrymen's tools that haunt the forest. They say the *ghosts* of those quarrymen also linger there. Some have reported the eerie sounds of voices, machines, or hammers hitting the stone. Others have said they felt like they were being watched or even touched by someone or something that they couldn't see. One hiker even reported being chased from the grounds by an angry ghost. Others said they saw spirits moving in a mist around the mounds of rock. So many people have reported odd experiences at the quarry that it is often included on lists of the most haunted hikes in New England.

If the quarry is haunted, it really wouldn't be a surprise. For so many years, men dug deep into the earth there. Who knows what dark and scary things may have come out of the ground with those stones?

The Phantom Train of Pittsfield

When a train passes by at night, it's a lot like a ghost. Think about it. First you hear a spooky sound. "*Whoooooo!*" Then, you see a bright light. Then, suddenly, there it is! The train appears. It passes powerfully by—the earthshaking rumble and scream of the wind almost otherworldly—and then, just like that, it's gone. Since trains are so much like ghosts, it makes sense that there are so many stories about ghost trains. And here in the

Berkshires, we have one of our own: the phantom train of Pittsfield.

In 1958, Pittsfield was buzzing with the news of an old-fashioned steam train that some said they'd seen pass through town on a railroad track hardly ever used. The owner and patrons of the Bridge Lunch Diner were the first to report it. From the window of the little lunch counter that then stood on a railway bridge downtown, they said they saw the steam engine pulling a baggage car, five or six coaches, and a coal car. It had been so clear, they could see the glowing embers from the fire powering the train. The strangest thing was that this kind of train was almost never used any longer. By that time, most steam engines had been replaced by much more modern locomotives. When people called the train company to report it,

the company said there had been no trains running on that track that day, and that steam trains like the one they described had not run in that region for *years*.

But that didn't stop people from seeing it. One month later, another group of patrons at the Bridge Lunch Diner said they saw the train speed by beneath the bridge. Even though the company still said there wasn't a train, the story spread through town. Everybody was talking about the phantom train. Some believed it was the ghost of a train that had crashed nearby in 1865. Others said it was a train that had been crushed by a collapsing bridge in 1893. But no one knew for sure.

Wherever it may have come from, it seems the ghost train passed through town only those two times. After 1958, people no longer said they saw it, and since then, there have been no new reports of a ghost train on that track. But the story of the phantom train still echoes like a distant whistle through the hills of Berkshire County.

The Ghostly Soldiers of South Lee

If you met a ghost while walking alone down a road at night, I bet you'd be pretty scared. But imagine how frightened you'd feel if you stumbled on hundreds of ghosts marching at you like an army of soldiers?

That's exactly what happened to a young Berkshire farmer named Caleb Hudson one stormy night during the Revolutionary War. That very night, Caleb stumbled into the South Lee

Inn. His eyes were wide, and he was out of breath.

"What's gotten into you, Caleb?" said Seth Deming, the man behind the bar. "You look like you've seen a ghost!"

A group of men who stood at the bar turned to look at the frightened farmer.

"Not just one," Caleb gasped.

"What do you mean?" asked one of the men.

But Caleb was too scared to say more.

"Sit down, Caleb," said Seth. "Sit down before you *fall* down."

The farmer sat down hard on a barstool as Seth handed him a mug of hot cider. Caleb took a deep drink and then a deep breath, and then at last he started to tell his tale.

"I was riding out of Lenox, down into South Lee, along the Housatonic River, when all of a sudden, my horse, Buckskin, stopped walking and started sniffing the air. I could tell that something was bothering him, so I patted his neck and said, 'What's the matter, boy?' But he just kept looking off down the road into the dark woods ahead. So, I looked where he was looking, and that's when I saw them."

"Saw who?" asked one of the men.

"They looked like soldiers, hundreds of soldiers, marching together. Left. Right. Left. Right. Down the road from Stockbridge."

"Was it the British?" asked Seth. At that time, the British and American armies were at war with each other. They were fighting over who should get to rule America. So, to see a group of British soldiers marching through the Berkshires, then, would have been scary—but it would not have been unusual.

"That's what I thought," said Caleb. "Must be the British. So, Buckskin and I hid in the bushes and waited for them to go by. But as they got closer, I could see they were American. They were wearing our uniform."

"So, did you jump up and greet them?" asked one of the men.

"Well, I was about to," said Caleb. "But just then, the strangest thing happened."

"What was it?" asked Seth.

"Well," Caleb continued, "just as I was about to stand up, the soldiers suddenly turned off the road and marched into the river. Now, there was nothing especially ghostly about that. Soldiers march through rivers all the time when the water is low enough, which it was right there by the crossing. But then I realized—all these men with their booted feet marching down the rocky road and splashing into the river—they didn't make a single sound. Not even a whisper. All I could hear was the rain falling and the river rushing by. And then . . ."

"What?" one man asked.

"Tell us!" another man shouted.

"Before they made it to the other side of the river, the entire army disappeared! Gone, just like that. Vanished in the night. And that's when I knew I had just seen an army of ghosts. My heart started pounding in my chest. *Thump. Thump. Thump.* I jumped up onto old Buckskin and tried to turn him around so we could get out of there before any more appeared. But the poor old horse was so scared, he bolted straight into the river—right through the place where the ghosts had been! We got through and kept on riding until we finally made it here to the inn."

After Caleb finished his story, the men sat quietly for a good long while. In the flickering light of the fire, they looked nervously through the windows, where the wind and rain lashed against the glass. Some thought they saw something moving out there, but they couldn't be sure it wasn't just their eyes playing tricks. Most of the men believed that what Caleb had seen that night were the ghosts of fallen American soldiers. They were so determined to protect their country that they marched from death, right back into battle.

The Ghost of Green River

During the Revolutionary War, the residents of Egremont were very afraid. Enemy soldiers had buried one of their dead in the local cemetery. People said his ghost was now haunting the town. They said it was seen floating among the tombstones or over the Green River, just beside the cemetery. One night, some men gathered there to investigate the sightings and try to prove they were untrue. But before long, something sent them running from the graveyard and into the village store across the road. There, they huddled around the wood stove, still too scared to speak.

The thin plank walls creaked as the wind swept along the road and through the leafless trees. The men sat quietly, listening to the knocks and creaks on the walls. Then Si Pickerel, the owner of the village store, stepped out slowly from behind the counter with a clay jug of hot cider in his hand.

"What happened out there?" he asked as he poured each man a mug. A wind gust rose suddenly and pushed against the door as if someone were outside trying to get in. They all looked nervously toward the door.

Finally, a skinny young man named Jed Tompkins started to speak. "We were . . ."

"Quiet, Jed," said Joe Tanner, a broad and burly man with a big black beard. Joe didn't believe in ghosts, and the last thing he wanted to do was scare everybody even further by telling tales.

But Jed stood up and shouted, "I have a right to speak, Joe, and you can't stop me! When I told you two nights ago that I saw a ghost down by the river, you said I was crazy. But now every man in Egremont knows that I was right and you were wrong, because we all saw the ghost tonight."

"I saw it, too," said one of the men. "And I, and I," said the others.

"We all saw it," said Jed as he turned toward Si. "We all saw it. We walked into the graveyard through the old iron gate. The clouds were passing over the moon, and we could see shadows moving on the tombstones and grass. At first, we thought they all were shadows. But then, right above that enemy soldier's grave, one of the shadows started to rise up from the ground. We could see that it was a man dressed in soldier's clothes with long black boots and gold buttons shimmering in the moonlight. We froze. We were so scared. Then, the ghost opened his mouth, raised his arms, and started reaching toward us. He looked like he was trying to say something, but he couldn't. He just looked at us. Oh, he had the saddest eyes I've ever seen. Then he turned and floated away toward the river. And that's when we ran right out of that graveyard."

"Is this true, Joe?" asked Si.

Joe didn't want to believe that there really was a ghost in town, but he saw it that night with his very own eyes, and he had to admit that Jed's story was true. So, he nodded his head slowly.

"Something must be done," he said. "We have to get rid of that ghost."

"Well, what should we do?" asked Si.

"We never should have let the enemy bury their dead in our graveyard," said Joe. "He doesn't belong here. That's why his ghost is wandering. He's trying to find a way out. I say we help him."

Jed looked nervously at Joe. "You don't mean..."

"I'm afraid that's exactly what he means," said Si. "He wants us to dig up that body and move it out of town."

"But wouldn't that be wrong?" asked Jed.

"It would be wrong to let that ghost keep scaring everybody senseless all over town," said Joe. "We have no choice! Let's go, men!"

They grabbed shovels and walked back over to the graveyard. With no sign of the ghost, they dug up the coffin and placed it onto the back of a wagon. As the night grew darker, they traveled north on Van Deusenville Road until they reached West Stockbridge, where they turned onto an old timber trail that ran up Tom Ball Mountain. They followed the trail to the place where the trees closed around them. When they could go no farther, they stopped the wagon in the deepest and darkest part of the woods. They thought they were all alone, but then Jed Tompkins saw a pale white light out of the corner of his eye.

"It's the ghost!" he screamed.

The men turned to look, and there on the coffin sat the ghostly soldier with his mouth hanging open and his arms reaching out. The men screamed and jumped off the wagon. But when they looked back, the ghost was gone. So, they quickly dug a hole and lowered the coffin into it, and as they tossed in the last of the dirt, they sighed. They thought they were finally rid of that troublesome spirit.

"There, that should put an end to it," said Joe.

Suddenly Jed screamed. "I'm not so sure about that, Joe. Look!"

The men looked back toward the lonely grave. And there beneath the branches, in the dim light of their torches, they saw the ghostly soldier rushing toward them through the trees. Terrified, they shrieked and leapt onto the wagon.

"Let's get out of here!" shouted Joe.

Jed cracked the whip over the horses and they burst into a run. The frightened company raced back down the mountain and were home before the sun came up.

From that day on, the ghost was never again seen in Egremont. But it was said that the people of West Stockbridge had now begun to see something strange in the woods near Tom Ball Mountain.

The Shadows of The Mount

When the famous author Edith Wharton was nine years old, she became very sick. After spending a long time resting, she began to feel much better, but then something she did made her sick again. She read a story. But this wasn't just any story. It was a ghost story. And after Wharton read it, not only did the sickness come back, but she also began to feel very afraid.

Everywhere she went, she felt like something was behind her, something dark like a shadow. She often felt it following her as she walked home through the woods, and sometimes she thought she saw it in the corner of the room. She was always afraid the shadow would catch her! She believed it was the ghost story that brought it into her life. In fact, she became so afraid of ghost stories that she would not sleep in a house if any of the books on any of the shelves had a ghost story in them. If she found one, she would burn it in the fireplace!

But Wharton didn't want to be afraid for the rest of her life, so, one day, she decided to do a very brave thing. She decided to start writing her own ghost stories. Maybe if she wrote about ghosts, she thought, she would know that it was only make-believe. Maybe then those stories wouldn't scare her anymore. And maybe then the shadow wouldn't get her. It seemed to work. Wharton wrote many ghost stories, and with each one she finished, she became less and less afraid.

But did the shadow ever go away? Maybe, but maybe not.

When Wharton was older, she built a beautiful house in the Berkshires that she named The Mount. For ten years, she lived in the house, and she wrote many books and stories there, including some of her ghost stories. No one knows whether Wharton ever saw the shadow at The Mount, but what we do know is that, ever since she moved away, many have said they have seen it there, from the students who lived in the house when it was a girls' boarding school right up to the workers and visitors of the museum that's there today. The shadow has been seen all over the house, on the walls and in the hallways and corners—even in someone's bedroom at night!

A man named Dennis woke one night to find a tall shadowy figure with a hood over its face standing beside his bed. Dennis tried to get up, but he couldn't move. It felt like something was holding him down! Finally, the shadow disappeared, and Dennis was able to sit up.

Another night, a cleaner once looked down the third-floor hallway and saw a very tall, thin shadow leaning out from a doorway. It seemed to look right at her! The cleaner was so scared that she dropped the vacuum on the stairs and ran right out of the house.

On Halloween in 2011, one of the museum's guides said she looked up at the wall of the den to see the shadow of a man standing right beside hers. But there was no one next to her. In fact, she was the only one in the entire house at the time! The figure leaned in close to her as she froze in fear. Then, suddenly, it moved away and disappeared. Another shadow man was seen drifting toward a guide outside one of the guest bedrooms upstairs. There was even a photograph taken in the drawing room of a shadow woman with a long, thin neck.

Probably the scariest encounter happened in the stable. There, on the top floor, a workman once said he looked into the corner and saw the shadow of a man crouching down and peering at him with glowing eyes. The workman dropped his tools and ran, and he never again went up to the top floor of the stable.

Eerie shadows are not the only strange things people have experienced at The Mount. Over the years, there have been reports of noises, smells, and sightings. But the shadow has been seen there so many times and by so many people that when people think of The Mount, they think of its moving shadows.

Could this be the very same shadow that once haunted Edith Wharton? Did it escape from the story that scared her as a child, and now no one can get it back into the book? No one knows for sure. But if you ever visit The Mount, keep your eyes open and watch out for moving shadows, especially if you've just been reading a book about ghosts!

A Little Girl Ghost and a Spooky Old Doll

On the second floor of Ventfort Hall Mansion and Gilded Age Museum, there is a room called the nursery, which many believe is haunted. In that room, the ghost of an old woman in a black veil was seen standing beside a crib. A rocking horse was spotted moving on its own, and a guest once felt her shirt tugged by someone she couldn't see.

But of all the spooky things that have been seen in that room, the spookiest of all may be the doll named Toddy. Toddy is very old. She was made more than one hundred years ago at a time when dolls were made with real human hair. So, the hair on the top of Toddy's little head was once on the head of someone now dead! But that's not all. Someone at the museum said she once found a doll's shoe lying on the floor by the door, far from where Toddy was. How could that shoe end up there, she wondered, unless the doll got up and walked across the room?

It may also be that Toddy was carried across the room by the ghost of a little girl who some have named Susie. While many believe that Susie's ghost haunts the nursery, they don't think she stays in that room. Though some have heard her voice there, others claim to have heard it in the dining room and in other rooms throughout the house. In one of the bedrooms, a museum guide once felt an icy cold spot in the air beside her. It stopped a few feet off the floor, at just about the height of a little child. The guide said she could feel it moving around her, from one side to the other. There was also a psychic in the room at the time, a person who can see and speak with spirits that others cannot see or hear. This psychic said she could see the ghost of a little girl walking around the guide. Wherever the guide felt the icy cold spot, she said, that's where the little girl was! Was it Susie? The psychic didn't know for sure, but they do think she's the only little girl ghost in the house.

No one seems to know who Susie was in life. Ventfort Hall was built in 1893, during what is known as the Gilded Age, by a man and a woman named George and Sarah Morgan. The Morgans did have three children, but by the time they moved into the house, their children were all grown up. None of them would have been as young as Susie the ghost is believed to be.

Susie is certainly not the only ghost haunting

Ventfort Hall. In fact, ghost hunters say there are so many spirits coming and going throughout the home that it is like a bus station for ghosts. Both George and Sarah Morgan are there, they believe. The scent of George's cigar is often detected in the library and the office. Many say Sarah's ghost appears when there are parties and other events at the house. Sometimes she is heard walking down the main hallway, and other times she is seen in the musician's gallery in the Great Hall. The story goes that Sarah loved to throw parties at the house when she was alive, and now, even as a ghost, she loves to play host.

Another ghost that has been seen in the Great Hall is an elderly woman dressed in old-fashioned clothing. When the house was used as a ballet school, some of the students used to see the old woman walking behind them in a mirror, but when they turned around to look, she was gone. Upstairs on the second floor, guides have heard the sound of footsteps and doors opening and closing on their own. Strange sounds reported in many parts of the house include a piano playing, dogs barking, whispers, screams, and even a growl.

But of all the spirits in all the rooms of this huge, haunted house, a little girl ghost named Susie, a doll known as Toddy, and the eerie little second-floor nursery are what seem to spook people the most.

Was Ashintully Cursed?

In the town of Tyringham, in a mansion known as Ashintully, lived a man named Robb de Peyster Tytus, who was famous for exploring the pyramids, the ancient tombs of Egyptian kings.

Some people called Ashintully "The Marble Palace" because it was made of marble, stucco, and white sand that sparkled in the sunlight and shimmered in the moonlight. People would pass by this palace on the hillside and stare up at it, all shimmering and shiny. Some said it was a magical place, but others called it cursed, on account of all the odd things that happened there.

Tytus was a world traveler and often not at home, but he liked to collect things he found in his travels and keep them in his mansion on the hill. Some said these objects made strange things happen in the house. Because, they said, some of the things that Tytus brought home were haunted.

One night, a man named Henry Adams, the great-grandson of President John Adams, was sleeping in a bedroom upstairs when he was startled awake by a voice whispering his name.

"Henry. Henry, wake up!"

Henry opened his eyes and looked around the room, and there on the wall, he saw a painting of a man in old Roman robes glowing with a pale blue light.

"Who's there?" Henry asked, afraid to hear the painting answer him. Whoever heard of a painting that could talk? But sure enough, the voice came again.

"Henry, come here. I want to talk to you."

"Go away," Henry said. "I'm sleeping. And anyway, paintings can't talk."

"I'm not a painting," the painting said.

"Then what are you? Who are you?" said Henry.

"My name is Lucius."

"Lucius? Lucius *who*?"

"Lucius Cornelius."

"Never heard of you," Henry said.

"I am a senator from Rome."

"That's impossible!" Henry shouted. "I must be dreaming."

With that, Henry closed his eyes and drifted off to sleep. And in the morning, the painting of the man in the Roman robes no longer glowed pale blue. But all throughout the day, Henry felt the painting's eyes follow him everywhere around the room.

Another day, something happened in the garden shed that scared the poor old gardener. He opened the door, and on the floor he found a body wrapped in ragged cloth! The old man screamed and ran for help. He brought back the sheriff, who called for a doctor, who examined the body and confirmed that the man was definitely dead. "But," he said, "this isn't a case of murder or foul play. This man has been dead for more than three thousand years!" It was a mummy that Tytus had taken from an Egyptian tomb. He had stored it in the shed and forgot to warn that unfortunate gardener!

Today, Ashintully is gone. The massive house was burned in a fire back in 1951, and all that remains are four cracked columns on a broken

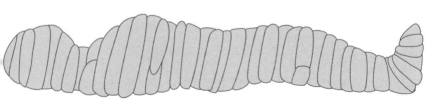

stone foundation. Some believe the fire that destroyed the estate wasn't an accident. It was, they say, the ghosts of those dead Egyptian kings who laid a curse upon that land, and on that man named Tytus who dared to disturb their sleep.

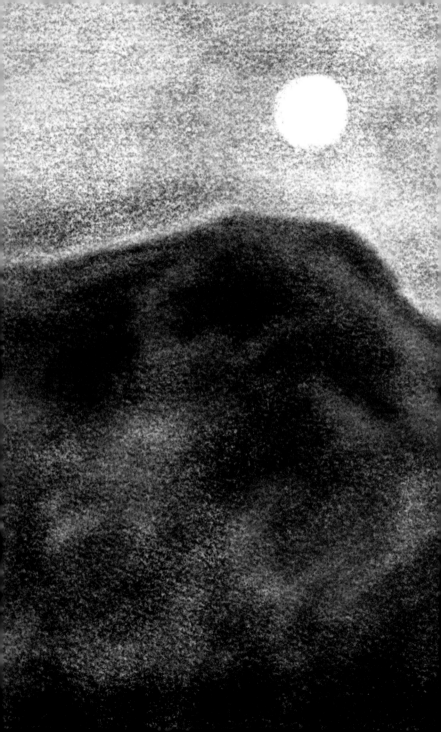

The Ghosts of October Mountain

Deep in the woods on October Mountain, there was once a large hunting lodge known as The Antlers. It was built by a man named William C. Whitney, who was the secretary of the United States Navy. Though Whitney already owned ten properties all over the world, he dreamed of having a place where he could hunt wild animals. So, in 1895, he bought the mountain. That's right—he bought the entire mountain. And he filled it with wild animals that he could hunt. There were buffalo, elk, antelope, sheep, pheasants, partridge, quail, rare black-tailed deer, angora goats, Belgian hares, and a pair of Canadian moose. And at the center of his private mountain-top hunting ground was his big, beautiful estate, which included not only the lodge, but a stable, water and observation towers, and a lakeside boathouse, too.

When Whitney died in 1904, his children took over the property, but they didn't want to live there, so they left it to fall apart. They did try to gather up all the animals, though. Many were sent to zoos and nature preserves. But some escaped and continued to live on the mountain for many years. One of the Canadian moose was often seen walking up the road in Lee and Lenox. He became so famous that people gave him the name "Old

Bill." Today, if you visit the Berkshire Museum, you can see Old Bill there, stuffed and mounted on the wall.

The Antlers burned down in the 1920s, and Whitney's old hunting ground became October Mountain State Forest. It's used today by hikers, hunters, campers, and nature lovers. But many people believe the entire mountain is haunted by ghosts and strange creatures and even visitors from outer space.

Once, long ago, a man claimed he had been attacked by giant vampire bats while out fishing on the mountain. Many tell stories of "horned devils" near Felton Lake. A "humanlike" creature with glowing eyes was reported in 1983 and again in 1989. Some say these creatures are only Whitney's wild animals still roaming around the mountainside. But others believe they are something supernatural. People say that Whitney himself haunts his old estate. His ghost has been seen moving from tree to tree with a lantern in his hand and a dog by his side, still hunting for those animals even in the afterlife.

The best-known ghost on October Mountain is a little girl named Anna Pease. People say she haunts "the lost cemetery" on West Branch Road. The cemetery isn't really lost. There's a sign nearby and a path that leads right to it. People still go there sometimes. But if you've never been there before, it can be hard to find, and sometimes people do lose their way. Sometimes they get so spooked trying to find it that they want to turn back and go home. After all, when you're out there in the woods up on the mountain, it's hard not to think about the stories you've heard.

As you drive into the woods along rocky, dirt roads, you'll feel like you're getting farther and farther away from anywhere people live. And as the dark woods surround you, you'll start to think about the ghost of Old Man Whitney, about the strange creatures, about eyes watching through tree trunks, and about lights in the sky at night.

But if you keep going, you'll find the "lost" cemetery. You'll see its crumbling stones in a small

grassy clearing surrounded by trees. You might catch the sun setting behind the trees and see one last golden shaft of light shine upon a broken tombstone. And if you walk over to get a better look at it, you'll see the faded name of Anna Pease, aged ten years, nine months, born on May 14, 1818, and buried on January 22, 1829. Maybe you won't feel afraid there. Maybe you'll feel calm; maybe even a little sad. If there are ghosts haunting this cemetery, maybe they just feel lonely out there in the woods. Maybe they just want someone to visit them.

The West Branch Road Cemetery has been there since the early 1800s, a time when farmers and woodcutters lived nearby. Back then, this spot would have been close to a village and would not have felt so far from daily life. But not many go there today. Every now and then, a hiker will pass through. Sometimes a local resident stops by. Ghost hunters come now and again to investigate the strange sightings and sounds that have been reported there. People say they have heard Anna's voice as she hums a distant tune. And they say they've seen her, too, a ghostly little girl dressed in white, walking through the trees and fallen stones. Maybe she's just looking for a friend. And maybe if you visit, you'll sit with her awhile and let her know you'll tell the world her story when you leave.

CHAPTER 14

Would You Stay in Room 301?

The Red Lion Inn in Stockbridge is one of the oldest inns in the Berkshires. Though the huge, white building that you see today was built only about 125 years ago, there was a tavern and an inn on that very same spot a very long time before. All the way back to the Revolutionary War, colonists used to gather at the tavern to talk about fighting the English. Travelers along the coach road outside would stop and stay the night at the inn. Since then, many people have stayed at the Red Lion, including some famous folks and several U.S. presidents.

But of all the guests who have stayed at the Red Lion Inn, the most famous of all is the ghost that haunts room 301. Many say they've met this ghost while sleeping there. Imagine you're just trying to get a good night's sleep when suddenly you feel something tugging on the sheets or your toes! Or something touches your face or scratches your hand or even climbs into bed with you! These are all things that people have reported after staying in room 301. And others said they actually *saw* it. They said it looked like a man in a top hat standing beside their bed.

Believe it or not, some people have actually chosen to stay in room 301, hoping to meet the ghost. Ghost hunters have brought all sorts of ghost detection devices with them to try to capture evidence, and a few said they did. One pair of ghost hunters said they recorded the sound of knocking coming from a dresser and later saw its doors open on their own. And in the middle of the night, they said they saw a hazy figure move across the room.

While room 301 does seem to be the most haunted room at the Red Lion, ghosts have been reported all over the inn. In room 424, one guest said something was standing near her bed, and another said they saw the ghost of a girl with flowers in her hand. Someone else felt something brush against her while she was walking downstairs into the parlor. According to the housekeepers, there are ghosts all over the fourth floor.

If you ask the owners of the Red Lion Inn whether any of these stories are true, they'll tell you they don't really know for sure. They'll invite you to stay overnight and find out for yourself. So, what do you think? Would you accept that invitation and maybe meet a ghost? Would you stay in room 301?

The Ghost of the Knox Trail Inn

It may be hard to imagine now, but many years ago, there were no houses in the Berkshires. No stores, hotels, or ski resorts. No hikers or bikers or leaf peepers. No motorboats or cars, and not a single highway. But there was a road, one road known by many names: the Great Road, the Post Road, and the Greenwoods Road, to mention only a few. Back then, that one road was the only way to travel safely through the Berkshires, a wooded wilderness filled with many dangers.

In the earliest days, the road was used by the Mohican people, whose home was here. Later, European settlers began to use it as they moved into the area and pushed the Mohicans out. During the Revolutionary War, soldiers also used the road as they marched from battle to battle. It was one of those Revolutionary War regiments and their

famous leader, a man named Henry Knox, that gave this road the name by which we know it today: Knox Trail.

Henry Knox was a general in the American army, who was fighting, then, against the British. Knox and his men had just captured a British fort at Ticonderoga, New York, and took cannons and other weapons from the fort. At that time, the British were also attacking the harbor out by Boston. General Knox knew that if he could get those cannons there, he could help his friends beat the British. So, Knox and his men dragged the heavy cannons all the way from Ticonderoga to Boston using this road, passing right through the Berkshires. This heroic act helped the Americans win the war. Because of that, the road was renamed the Knox Trail after General Henry Knox.

The Knox Trail still winds through the woods here in the Berkshires. You can find part of it out in Otis. But don't expect to see anything like a modern-day highway. It can be hard to spot among the trees, leaves, and boulders. If you look, though, you'll find some signs near the forest that mark its location.

Not far from the Knox Trail, you'll find the Knox Trail Inn, which some believe is haunted by the ghosts of those same men who dragged the heavy cannons across the wilderness all those years ago. People say that on certain nights you can hear what sounds like men dragging something heavy, like a cannon, past the building. Inside the inn, the ghost of a soldier has been spotted. Some say he came from the Revolutionary War, but others say he looked like a much more modern ghost, as if he fought in the Civil War or maybe World War I.

People there call the ghost Jake, and they say that he can be a real troublemaker. A former owner of the inn said she once heard noises coming from the barroom, and she ran in expecting to find kids trying to steal something from behind the bar. But what she found instead was the ghost of a blonde-haired man wearing a green army jacket staring at the fireplace. When she yelled out, "I gotcha now," the man walked toward the door and disappeared.

Another time she found all the candles in the barroom lit, even though she was the only person at the inn that night and she hadn't lit them. She blew them out and went up to bed. But when she came back downstairs a little bit later, she found them all lit again. Then she yelled at the ghost, "Stop it! You're gonna burn the place down!" And it never happened again.

A woman whose family used to live at the inn said they always woke up at four o'clock in the morning because they could hear someone walking around in the attic. She also said that she once woke up in the middle of the night to find the blonde-haired ghost standing in her room next to her bed. The man turned to walk toward her and then vanished. She said they never felt afraid of Jake. They felt that he just wanted to be part of their family.

But the people who work at the Knox Trail Inn today say that Jake has become more of a troublemaker than he ever was before. One guest of the inn reported seeing plates flying through the air, as well as toilet paper unrolling on its own. Some of the workers have said they felt something tugging on their hair or pulling on their aprons, and they once saw a water glass crash to the floor in the kitchen. People have heard voices speaking and music playing, have felt cold spots, and have seen shadow figures and faces moving around.

The people at the Knox Trail Inn blame the hauntings on the ghost they call Jake, though no one knows for sure who Jake was, or where and when he came from. But it's possible that this blonde-haired man in a green army uniform once helped Henry Knox drag heavy cannons across the Berkshires, so they could win the battle against the British out in Boston Harbor.

Haunted Highwood Manor

From where they sat on the porch of Highwood Manor, on the grounds of Tanglewood, the kids could see down to the lake called Stockbridge Bowl and the little red farmhouse beside it. It was late September and the leaves had started to turn. Everywhere the bursts of red and yellow were like little fairy fires in the green treetops. White mist drifted like a ghost above the meadow, gliding from the lakeshore to the back porch where the group sat waiting for the story to begin. On the top stair sat the storyteller, a tall young man with a quick, bright gleam in his nut-brown eyes.

"Did you know this is a haunted house?" he asked, and as soon as he said it, he knew his audience was in the palm of his hand. After all, who doesn't want to hear about a ghost?

"Oh really?" asked one of the girls. She never believed in ghosts, and she wasn't about to start now.

"Oh yes," said the young man. "There are many stories about this house. People have witnessed all sorts of strange things."

"Like what?" asked the doubtful girl.

"Like cold air out of nowhere, or water running in the bathroom sink," answered the storyteller. "Doors opening and closing or lights switching on and off. And then there are the sounds."

"What kind of sounds?" asked a little boy in a trembling voice.

"The sound of someone breathing or the footsteps on the floor upstairs," said the storyteller. "But of all the things that people have experienced here, it's the feeling of being touched that scares them the most."

"Touched?" the boy gulped. "By a ghost?"

"That's right," the storyteller said. "Someone once said she felt her hair lifted right up off her shoulders by someone she couldn't see! And of course, everyone who goes into this house is afraid of the second floor. No one wants to go up there."

The kids looked up at the windows above the striped awnings overhead. Even on this breezy, sunny morning, those windows seemed extra dark and super spooky. Someone said they thought they saw a face in the glass. Or was it only their eyes playing tricks?

"Whose ghost is it?" asked one of the older boys. He was curious about the history of the house and property. "Was it someone who lived here?"

"No one knows for sure," said the storyteller. "But some believe it's the ghost of a man named Oreb Andrews who worked on this property many years ago, even before this house was built, when all of this land was a farm. They say old Oreb was killed by a falling tree one stormy night and was buried nearby. There he lay quiet until, many years later, some workmen moved his tombstone while clearing the land to make room for a parking lot. That's when the ghost of Oreb Andrews rose from his grave and went looking for those who dared to disturb him."

"What about the people who built this house?" asked the curious boy.

"Well, that would be Samuel Gray Ward and his wife, Anna," answered the storyteller. "He was a banker from Boston and a part-time poet. He and Anna built the place in 1844 and lived here for a few years until they had to move back to Boston so that Samuel could take care of his sick father. Then, their friends, William and Caroline Tappan, moved in, and they rented out that little red farmhouse down there to Nathaniel Hawthorne."

"Who's that?" asked the boy.

"He was a famous author," said the storyteller. "He's the one who came up with the name Tanglewood, which is what they call this whole place today. And he wrote some of his books right there in that farmhouse, including one called *The Wonder Book*. In that one, there's a young man who tells stories to a group of kids right here on this porch."

"Hey, that's like us," said the boy.

"It's exactly like us," the storyteller said.

"Are we in a story?" asked a little girl, looking around.

"Ah, my dear girl, life is a story," answered the storyteller with a wink.

"So, do the Tappans haunt the house?" asked the curious boy.

"As I said, no one knows," answered the storyteller. "But one thing they do say about the Highwood ghost is that it seems to be especially fond of music and musicians. Are any of you musicians?"

A few of the children raised their hands.

"Well, keep your eyes open," said the storyteller. "Because you may see something that no one else can see. That's exactly what happened to Leonard Bernstein, you know."

"Who's that?" someone asked.

"He was a famous composer of music," answered the storyteller. "He used to work right here in this house, upstairs."

"On the second floor?" asked the little boy with the trembling voice.

"The very same," the storyteller said. "Bernstein had an office up there."

"What was he doing working in someone else's house?" asked the doubtful girl.

"Well, you see," answered the storyteller,

"By that time, the house was no longer anyone's home. It had been given to the Boston Symphony Orchestra, so they could use it during their summer music festival, which they still do today. For a few years right before he died, Leonard Bernstein used to stay here and work on his music right up there where no one liked to go. And people said that he had more than one encounter with the Highwood ghost up there. Once, they said, he suddenly stood up from his chair and shouted, 'What is it that's there? Who is it that's there?' as he looked up at the ceiling. He seemed to see something there that no one else could see. And another time, as he was walking up the stairs, he turned to his friend and said, 'This place is haunted.' They said he even went up into the attic late one night to play music for the ghost, hoping it would make the spirit appear. It didn't appear that night, but Bernstein did say he once saw it walking along the back of the stage over in the concert hall during a performance."

"But who was it?" asked the boy who was curious about history.

"Some said it was the ghost of a man named Serge Koussevitzky, one of the founders of the music festival," answered the storyteller. "But there are those who say the spirit is a child, and when other children are around, especially if they are also musicians, his ghost comes out to play."

"You're just trying to scare us," said the doubtful girl. "It's only a story."

"You may be right," said the storyteller. "It might all be just a story. But then again, maybe stories are more real than you think, and maybe ghosts are closer than you know. You may have even met one today."

Suddenly, a breeze blew through the nearby treetops, and all eyes looked away from the storyteller toward the falling leaves and the mist in the meadow. Then, they noticed that his voice had grown quiet. When they looked back to where the storyteller had been, they realized he was gone.

A Ghostly Goodbye

Well done, my friends. You made it through this journey into the shadows of the Berkshires. I hope your trusty flashlight served you well. Now that you've finished this book, I hope you'll continue to read all about this special part of New England and maybe even visit some of these places yourself. And should you see or hear or feel anything strange out there, be sure to tell a story of your own. Who knows? Maybe your story will one day take its place among the ghostly tales of the Berkshires.

Ever since he was a kid growing up in northern New Jersey, **Robert Oakes** has loved to write songs and tell stories. But it wasn't until he started leading ghost tours at The Mount in Lenox, MA, that he became especially interested in the spooky side of life. Since then, Robert has published two books about ghost stories and haunted places and has offered many ghost tours and paranormal presentations. Robert also loves to teach literature and writing. He currently serves as associate director of communications at Rectory School in Pomfret, CT. For more information about Robert and his work, visit robertoakes.net.

Katherine Oakes was born and raised in the Quiet Corner of Northeastern Connecticut where, as a child, she spent most of her free time drawing and painting while also taking lessons with local artists. Years later, Katherine earned her bachelor's degree in studio painting from Bard College at Simon's Rock in the Berkshires of Western Massachusetts and also took part in the Guild of Berkshire Artists. She has shown her work at numerous juried art shows and fairs throughout New England and offers it for sale under Hazelwood Arts on Etsy. Last year, Katherine moved back to her hometown of Pomfret, CT, to teach elementary and middle school art at Rectory School. For more information about Katherine and her work, visit katherineoakesart.com.

Check out some of the other *Spooky America* titles available now!

Spooky America was adapted from the creeptastic *Haunted America* series for adults. *Haunted America* explores historical haunts in cities and regions across America. Here's more from the original *Ghosts of the Berkshires* author, Robert Oakes:

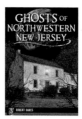

robertoakes.net
katherineoakesart.com